CONTENTS

INTRODUCTION

I decided to take a "Women Gender Studies" course in my sophomore year of college. My instructor asked the class as a whole how many of us considered ourselves a feminist. As you may have guessed, not many of us raised our hands. However, when the professor raised the question if men and women should be treated equally, the majority of the class raised their hands. Essentially, the professor asked the class if we were feminists and then asked us if we believed what feminists believe. So, why was there a disparity in the number of people who raised their hands? Shouldn't they be treated as the same question? After all, if we agree with what feminists fight for, why not take up the label as a feminist ourselves?

The simple fact that not every hand went up demonstrates that sexism is still an issue today. Moreover, why did so few of us identify as feminists, but so many of us agree on equality of the sexes? Outside of the classroom, the answer is very clear. Feminist movements are generally agreeable, but the word "feminist" seems to raise alarms. Unfortunately, the "feminist" label carries with it a few negative perceptions and connotations, so it only makes sense that some people would want to avoid calling themselves a feminist.

WHAT IS A FEMINIST?

If you look up the word feminist in the dictionary, the term defines one as an advocate for women's equal rights and interests. All too often, people think feminists are fighting to suppress men.

Feminism is the belief that men and women should have the same opportunities regardless of gender.

I want to stress that feminism doesn't mean that "Oh, so now I can hit a woman if she hits me?" (a sentiment I've heard all too commonly, often said by men who just can't seem to understand what it is that feminists want). First of all, why do their minds go directly to physical violence? Second of all, feminism means having the same cerebral opportunities, such as being considered for the same job positions and not being confined to stereotypes typically associated with womanhood. Feminists are fighting for equality, not identicalness.

As it turns out, feminism goes all the way back to the 1700s. Actually, the earliest presence of feminist ideas, despite the term being coined later in history, is during ancient times. During this time period, women were merely decoration for a man, an extension of his beliefs, life, and identity. The belief that women were inferior to men was reflected in the laws and social norms of the time. We know that women possess equal intelligence, poise, strength, and determination. But in a patriarchal society–this information did not matter.

What does it mean to live in a patriarchal society? Well, patriarchy simply means "rule of the father," so living in a patriarchal society means that the majority of decision-making and power rests, for the most part, in the hands of men. Of course, living in a patriarchal society doesn't mean that women hold absolutely no positions of power or are powerless. It means that the overwhelming majority of power belongs to men, which is true of nearly all societies. Living in a patriarchal society has implications related to how women are treated, such as the presence of gender micro-aggressions and harmful stereotypes.

Clearly, society has come a long way from the 18th century. Thankfully, the period of women not having the right to vote or make decisions without their husband's consent are behind us. Similarly, women now have opportunities to join the workforce, and men are no longer the sole breadwinners of the family. Despite the constant opposition and barriers it has faced throughout the course of history, the feminist movement is still going strong today. However, we have some way to go in terms of progress for women of all races, sexualities, and classes before feminism can reach complete intersectionality.

Feminist movements have allowed young girls to grow up and make choices for themselves. There are three feminism waves that have been identified in United States History. There is still debate over whether we are currently living through the third wave of feminism or the fourth wave of feminism. Before the waves, which begin starting in 1848, there were feminist notions and opinions circulating public thought and making differences in the lives of ancient women around the world.

Feminist ideas can be traced all the way back to the ancient world.

Though the term "feminist" wasn't coined until 1837 (socialist Charles Fourier created the word to describe his utopian vision for the future, one in which women would have full freedom and equality), history's first feminists can be thought of as the women who lived during the earliest centuries, when the date was followed by BCE. There are records that show proof of a huge protest that took place in ancient Greece, where women fought for the right to possess expensive items like gold. Oppian Law had restricted such things, and influential leaders such as Roman consul Marcus Porcius Cato had supported and even advocated for the establishment of the law. The hoards of women fighting for their right to own certain kinds of property had prompted Cato to famously yell, "As soon as they begin to be your equals, they will have become your superiors!" It is astonishing to me how, hundreds of years later, essentially the same argument is being used to combat the feminist movement. The harmful stereotypes and baseless fears can be traced back through time, all the way to the ancient world.

The Middle Ages were rife with misogyny and gender roles. Women could either become a wife and mother or take a vow to become a nun. The roles of women in society were most commonly related to home and domestic matters. They were viewed as inferior to men and were only granted true power if they were born into a royal family. There were a few women who lived during this time period whose fight against gender discrimination was documented and preserved. Writer and poet Christine de Pisan was the very first feminist philosopher. Her works championed women and fought against the patriarchal norms of the Middle Ages. One of her most influential works, *The Book of the City of Ladies*, contained tales of heroic women and confronted the prevalent misogyny of 15th century France. The sequel, *Book of Three Virtues*, provided ancient women with a set of rules to follow to succeed in their prescribed societal roles.

There were a few notable advocates for feminism between

the Middle Ages and the Enlightenment. 15th-century Venetian scholar Laura Cereta focused on efforts related to women's right to an education and explored the prevalent abuse of women in marriages. She was often mocked and ridiculed for her progressive beliefs. Many people accused her of plagiarizing her works because they were too intellectual to have been written by a woman. Cereta clapped back at her overwhelmingly male critics, writing, "You brashly and publicly not merely wonder but indeed lament that I am said to possess as fine a mind as nature ever bestowed upon the most learned man. You seem to think that so learned a woman has scarcely before been seen in the world. You are wrong on both counts."

The Enlightenment took place during the 18th century and was a time period filled with radical change, scientific discovery, and profound thinking. The Enlightenment also saw the fight for the liberation of women begin to accelerate, mainly due to the emerging voices of early feminists such as Mary Wollstonecraft and Olympe de Gouges. Wollstonecraft's *A Vindication of the Rights of Woman*, the work for which she is best known for, argues for the equal treatment of women and men when it comes to education, and De Gouges' *Declaration of the Rights of Woman and of the Female Citizen* was so forward-thinking in its ideas of gender equality that it eventually led to the playwright's execution.

The efforts of these courageous women lead us to First-wave feminism, which took place (roughly) from 1848 to 1920. This initial wave centered around women's suffrage, which is the right for women to vote. First-wave feminism kicked off in 1848 with the first-ever women's rights convention to take place in the United States, called the Seneca Falls Convention. The convention was coordinated by abolitionists and activists Lucretia Mott and Elizabeth Cady Stanton. On the first day of the Seneca Falls Convention, Mott and Stanton read from their work titled "Declaration of Sentiments and Grievances," in which they amended the famous line from the Declaration of Independence, changing it to include women: "We hold these truths to be self-evident: that all men and women are created equal; that they are endowed by their Creator with certain inalienable rights..."

On the second day of the convention, one of the notable attendees was African-American abolitionist leader Frederick Douglass, who was one of the very few men in attendance. While in Seneca, Douglass voiced his support for the women's suffrage movement, going so far as to say that women's equality to men is innate, that "it is inscribed upon all the powers and facilities of her soul, and no custom, law or usage can ever destroy it." Douglass became one of the mere thirty-two male signees of Mott and Stanton's "Declaration of Sentiments and Grievances."

The fight for women's right to vote continued for over seventy years, slowed down slightly by both the Civil War and World War I, before it was finally granted in 1920 as the 19th amendment to the constitution. Thus, the fight for women's equality moved onwards towards Second-wave feminism.

However, before we can move onto Second-wave feminism, there are two important historical events that need to be discussed: the Great Depression and World War II. The Great Depression occurred from 1929 to 1933 and was characterized by high unemployment rates and decreasing gross domestic product across the globe. Despite the high unemployment rate and lack of job openings, the employment rate for women actually increased. Because their male counterparts had lost their jobs, women were needed in the workforce. Furthermore, the industries hit the hardest by the depression were generally male-dominated, so "women's work" like teaching, nursing, and paid housework was more widely available.

World War II took place from 1939 to 1945. With the majority of working-aged men off at war, there were a variety of work positions up for the taking. Women were finally able to break into spheres that were typically restricted to male workers, such as the mining industry and professional sports. Rosie the Riveter became a feminist icon as a result of the influx of working women, cheering them on with her slogan, "We Can Do It!" Even with the changing attitudes towards women in the workplace, women were still paid far less for their work than men in the same position. This wage gap led to the formation of the Equal Pay Act of 1963, which was one of the first attempts at getting rid of wage inequality and served as the first landmark of Second-wave feminism.

Second-wave feminism runs from the 1960s to the 1980s, though there is still discourse around the exact timetable of each of the feminism waves. American journalist and activist Betty Friedan became one of the leaders of Second-wave feminism. Her book *The Feminine Mystique*, published in 1963, is largely credited with putting Second-wave feminism into motion. *The Feminine Mystique* came to fruition after Friedan surveyed fellow Smith College graduates, asking if they found fulfillment in their roles as homemakers. When she discovered that other women had been feeling frustrated with the limitations that came along with their gendered roles, she began to work on what would become *The Feminine Mystique.* The best-selling nonfiction book challenges the idea that household work is guaranteed to bring women happiness, more so than if women were to do work outside of their domestic chores. It criticizes the work of controversial psychoanalysis founder Sigmund Freud, who once said that "nature has determined woman's destiny through beauty, charm, and sweetness. Law and custom have much to give women that has been withheld from them, but the position of women will surely be what it is: in youth an adored darling and in mature years a loved wife." Friedan pointed out that sentiments such as these feed into the notion of the feminine mystique, which is the idea that a woman's place in society is in the home. Through her writings, Friedan was able to gain the attention of politicians, lawmakers, and the general public, ushering in a new age of the feminist movement.

Betty Friedan further cemented her place in women's history when she co-founded the National Organization for Women (NOW) in 1966 with fellow feminists Shirley Chisholm, Pauli Murray, and Muriel Fox, among others, subsequently serving as the organization's first president. Both the success of *The Feminine Mystique* and the enactment of the Civil Rights Act of 1964 paved the way for the National Organization for Women's existence. Since its inception, the National Organization for Women has worked to pass anti-discrimination laws, advocate for the Equal Rights Amendment, and end violence against women.

Initially called the Lucretia Mott Amendment, the Equal Rights Amendment was first introduced in 1923 by feminist and gender equality activist Alice Paul. She presented the legislation at the Women's Rights Convention in Seneca Falls, saying: "If we keep on this way they will be celebrating the 150th anniversary of the 1848 Convention without being much further advanced in equal rights than we are...If we had not concentrated on the Federal Amendment we should be working today for suffrage...We shall not be safe until the principle of equal rights is written into the framework of our government."

The Equal Rights Amendment was accepted by both the Republican and Democratic parties in the 1940s, but it wasn't until 1972 that it became officially ratified by the majority of the states. To this day, there are still states that have yet to ratify the seemingly no-brainer amendment. Initially, the Equal Rights Amendment didn't get enough states to ratify within the proposed time limit. Congress has since lifted the time limit, and, last year, Virginia finally began to begin the process of ratification.

Betty Friedan was quite prolific during Second-wave feminism, and, with the help of women's rights activists Gloria Steinem and Bella Abzug, created the National Women's Political Caucus in 1971. This organization supports women who run for office by recruiting, training, and educating them before and during their political endeavors. Both the National Organization for Women and the National Women's Political Caucus are still making a difference today.

Another major milestone of Second-wave feminism was the publication of the first feminist magazine. Journalist and social political activist Gloria Steinem co-founded the *Ms.* magazine with African-American author Dorothy Pitman Hughes in 1972. The magazine's very first cover featured an illustration of an eight-armed pregnant woman. In her hands, she holds different items, each signifying a different facet of a woman's life. The goal of the cover was to show that women don't have to be confined to one type of job, lifestyle, or interest. Despite the box that society often puts them in, women can be versatile and complex in their many pursuits of fulfillment. Steinem's contributions to the feminist movement are explored briefly in FX's miniseries *Mrs. America*, where she is portrayed by actress Rose Byrne. Betty Friedan, mentioned previously, is also characterized in the show, and is played by Tracey Ullman.

One year after the Equal Rights Amendment was ratified, The U.S. Supreme Court took up the Roe v. Wade case and decided to grant women the right to an abortion. This landmark case began when Texas native Norma McCorvey was unable to get an abortion due to her state's strict reproductive laws, which stated that an abortion could only be performed if the procedure was necessary to save the life of the mother. It, allegedly, didn't even allow an abortion for women who were victims of rape or incest. McCorvey ended up winning the case and the Supreme Court ruled that women have the right to choose whether or not to have an abortion, and that doing so was one of their constitutional rights. The official wording of Roe v. Wade is as follows: "A person may choose to have an abortion until a fetus becomes viable, based on the right to privacy contained in the Due Process Clause of the Fourteenth Amendment." However, there were still some restrictions set in place depending on the trimester of pregnancy that the mother is in at the time of the abortion. Abortion was completely legal in the first trimester and was subject to more scrutiny during the second trimester, with the strictest laws relating to the third trimester. The Supreme Court left it up to the individual states to decide to what extreme they would try to prohibit and regulate the number of abortions.

Third-wave feminism emerged in the 1990s and focused on reclaiming the feminine identity and making feminism completely intersectional. Intersectional feminism is a term that was coined by American lawyer and scholar Kimberlé Williams Crenshaw in her 1989 paper, "Demarginalizing the Intersection of Race and Sex: A Black Feminist Critique of Antidiscrimination Doctrine, Feminist Theory and Antiracist Politics." Crenshaw describes intersectionality as it relates to feminism as "a prism for seeing the way in which various forms of inequality often operate together and exacerbate each other."

The first and second waves of feminism lacked intersectionality, mainly benefitting straight, college-educated white women and ignoring the needs of women of color, queer women, and women of the lower class. The dire need for intersectionality was apparent from feminism's earliest days. In 1851, American abolitionist and women's rights activist Sojourner Truth voiced her frustrations with the predominantly white-centered feminism in her famous "Ain't I a Woman?" speech, which would later be identified as one of the first calls for intersectionality. Additionally, suffragettes Susan B. Anthony and Elizabeth Cady Stanton refused to prioritize the fight for black men's right to vote before white women were granted the same ability. This is a prime example of white feminism. Anthony and Stanton put feminism and racism at odds with one another when, in reality, both issues need to be explored together, as if they are intertwined. During Second-wave feminism, American author Gloria Jean Watkins, better known by her pen name bell hooks (she chooses to write her name in lowercase to place less emphasis on her identity, more emphasis on her intellectual ideas), criticized the feminist movement's exclusivity to white women and urged those who wanted to participate in feminism to consider the struggles of women of all races, sexualities, ethnicities, and classes.

In addition to expanding the fight for women's equality to be more intersectional, Third-wave feminism explored womanhood and the feminine identity. The 1990s saw more women embracing their femininity and reclaiming gendered pejoratives such as "slut" and "whore," taking words historically used to degrade women and wearing them proudly.

The Riot Grrrl movement was one of the landmarks of Third-wave feminism. Originating in Olympia, Washington, the underground feminist movement emerged in the early 90s and challenged society's idea of what a woman should be. Its first manifesto reads, "Us girls crave records and books and fanzines that speak to us that we feel included in and can understand in our own ways. We are angry at a society that tells us Girl = Dumb, Girl = Bad, Girl = Weak." And so, members of the Riot Grrrl movement reclaimed what it meant to be a girl. They took the word "girl" and replaced the "i" with "rr," making the word resemble a growl of defiance and power. The girls were ready to riot, teeth bared and microphones in hand.

The Riot Grrrl consisted of punk bands that explored feminist themes in their art. Rape, queerness, fighting the patriarchy - no subject was too taboo or too complex to be included in the bands' music. Some of the most popular musical groups that participated in the Riot Grrrl movement were Bikini Kill, Bratmobile, Babes in Toyland, and Huggy Bear. Though they all faced heavy criticism from the public for being "too much," the bands of the Riot Grrrl movement continued to make music that defied harmful stereotypes and brought attention to issues associated with intersectional feminism for many decades.

Third-wave feminism was characterized by a newfound boldness, honesty, and candidness not previously seen in the first two waves. This is extremely apparent in one of the most recognized and celebrated contributions to Third-wave feminism: *The Vagina Monologues*. Written by V (formerly Eve Ensler), *The Vagina Monologues* is a political piece of theater meant to explore women's relationships with their vaginas. The play started with V having conversations with other women about their vaginas. When asked why she thought that so many women were eager to talk about something so personal, V replied, "Because no one's ever given them the opportunity to talk. Any time we open the door to a place where we have a lot of feelings or thoughts or stories, we react enthusiastically. The story of your vagina is the story of your life, and women want to talk about their lives." Some of the subjects the celebrated piece touches on are sex and sex work, sexual trauma, and childbirth. *The Vagina Monologues* seeks to empower women by encouraging a healthy relationship with their vaginas, sexuality, and womanhood. It entered new territory, one in which all women-identifying people were told to be proud of what made them women.

The world of entertainment and art continued to see new groups of activists working to combat all forms of oppression. The Guerrilla Girls were founded in 1985 as a response to the low percentage of female artists on display at the Museum of Modern Art's exhibition titled "An International Survey of Recent Painting and Sculpture," which featured the work of 152 male artists and only 13 female artists. The blatant exclusion of female artists ironically came at a time when the majority of figures depicted in art were of the female form, typically nude and typically objectified through the male gaze. Not only did the Museum of Modern Art disproportionately display pieces constructed by men, but the museum also lacked representation of artists of color.

Since 1985, the Guerrilla Girls have protested the sexism and racism that runs rampant in the art world, posting provocative posters around cities, educating the public on gender inequality in pop culture and art, and exhibiting female artists in predominantly male-populated art museums. The leaders of the Guerrilla Girls choose to remain anonymous, so they donned gorilla masks to conceal their identities. "The art world is a very small place. Of course, we were afraid that if we blew the whistle on some of its most powerful people, we could kiss off our art careers. But mainly, we wanted the focus to be on the issues, not on our personalities or our own work," said one of the founders. When asked why they chose gorilla masks, a Guerrilla Girl said, "We were Guerrillas before we were Gorillas. From the beginning, the press wanted publicity photos. We needed a disguise. No one remembers, for sure, how we got our fur, but one story is that at an early meeting, an original girl, a bad speller, wrote 'Gorilla' instead of 'Guerrilla.' It was an enlightened mistake. It gave us our 'maskulinity.'"

Though the timeline of the third and fourth waves of feminism have been long debated, it is generally accepted that Fourth-wave feminism began around 2012 and lasted throughout the 2010s. The concerns of this fourth wave of feminism largely center around rape culture, sexual harassment in the workplace, and furthering and maintaining intersectionality. The #MeToo movement, the Women's March's alignment with the Trump administration, and the Time's Up movement are significant markers of Fourth-wave feminism.

Activist Tarana Burke founded the Me Too movement in 2006 as a way to raise awareness of the all-too-common sexual violence and sexual harassment experienced by people around the world. It wasn't until October of 2017, when allegations of sexual misconduct against former American film producer and convicted sex offender Harvey Weinstein became widespread, that the Me Too movement went viral and gained instant popularity.

The Me Too movement relaunched after actress Alyssa Milano posted to her Twitter, "If all the women who have been sexually harassed or assaulted wrote 'Me too' as a status, we might give people a sense of the magnitude of the problem." This came shortly after Harvey Weinstein was exposed for sexually abusing women in the film industry. What followed is often referred to as the "Weinstein Effect," in which allegations of sexual abuse and harassment against powerful men were divulged and used to take them out of positions of power.

Milano's tweet was met with an outpouring of stories, receiving hundreds of thousands of replies before the day was over. Prominent Hollywood figures like Reese Witherspoon, Terry Crews, Jennifer Lawrence, and America Ferrera have voiced their support for the movement, coming forward about their personal experiences with sexual assault. Actress Gabrielle Union pointed out that, while she supports the movement itself, it has far to go in terms of its intersectionality. "I think the floodgates have opened for white women," she said in a New York Times article. "I don't think it's a coincidence whose pain has been taken seriously. Whose pain we have shown and continue to show. Whose pain is tolerable and whose pain is intolerable. And whose pain needs to be addressed now."

The 2017 Women's March took place one day after Donald Trump's Presidential Inauguration and happened around the globe. To this day, it holds the record for the largest single-day protest in United States history. The central protest - referred to as the Women's March on Washington - drew crowds of nearly half a million people, and the protest's total attendance was about 5 million across nearly 600 national cities.

Donald Trump's presidential campaign was tainted by misogynistic ideas and riddled with anti-women remarks, one of which went viral in a leaked video where Trump brags about grabbing women by the pussy. After Trump defeated Hillary Clinton in the 2016 elections, the plans for having a Women's March were pushed into overdrive. The purpose of the march was to "send a bold message to our new administration on their first day in office, and to the world that women's rights are human rights."

Women and men took to the streets on January 21, 2017. They held signs and posters that advocated for reproductive rights, LGBTQ+ rights, and any other human rights issues that were seemingly opposed by the Trump administration. However, Women's March co-founder Tamika Mallory made sure that the intentions of the march weren't construed incorrectly. "This effort is not anti-Trump. This is pro-women. This is a continuation of a struggle women have been dealing with for a very long time. In this moment, we are connecting and being as loud as possible."

Notable speakers at the event included political activist Angela Davis, multi-talented entertainer Janelle Monáe, and current United States Vice President Kamala Harris. The Pussyhat Project, in which women wore crocheted pink cat-like hats to reclaim the often derogatory word "pussy," was one of the various independent efforts present at the march. Another was the Art of Activism series at Studio Two Three, where people could make, buy, or design their own political screen prints.

Throughout history, those that call themselves feminists have fought for different things at different times. Whether it be for the right to own property in ancient times or for less sexual harassment in the workplace in modern times, feminism's cause has always had two things in common: women's liberation and women's equality. No matter what wave feminists have found themselves in, they are either fighting to break free of stereotypes or to take one more step towards complete and unequivocal equality, and most of the time both fights are fought simultaneously.

So, what does it mean to be a feminist in 2021? Being a feminist today means combatting gender microaggressions, seeking to bridge the gender pay gap, and ensuring that women of all races, sexualities, and classes have equal opportunities to men. Gender microaggressions are the seemingly harmless ideas expressed in verbal or written communication that have negative long-term effects on girls. One example of a gender microaggression is the saying, "Boys with be boys," which contributes to rape culture and excuses boys for bad behavior.

The gender pay (or wage) gap has been an issue prominent in media for quite some time. In 2020, it was reported that women earned 84% of what men earned, a number that is surely less for women of color. Still, there are people, mostly men, who believe that the wage gap isn't real. They dismiss that issue as being made up in order to serve a political motive. There have been published surveys in which nearly half of the men surveyed believed that the wage gap doesn't exist. The majority of women who participated in the survey, however, insisted that the wage gap is a real thing that desperately needs to be addressed. The differences in wages earned by men and women are a result of many complex factors, such as workplace discrimination, the societal expectation that women must stay home to take care of their children, and the undervaluation of traditionally female skills. Men shouldn't get to just sit back and let women do all the heavy lifting. In the words of Queen Bey, "Men have to demand that their wives, daughters, mothers, and sisters earn more—commensurate with their qualifications and not their gender. Equality will be achieved when men and women are granted equal pay and equal respect."

The principal goal in the 2020s is to have feminism be undoubtedly intersectional. Though some may argue that feminism is no longer needed, mostly due to the notion that women have already been granted the same rights as men, we still have long ways to go before these gender-based biases and microaggressions have been eradicated from society.

It is astounding to look back on this country's history of feminism - how far we've come as a society and all of the good that feminism has done for women - and realize that there are people who still believe that feminism shouldn't exist. Hearing the term "feminism" or "feminist" incites a deep rage inside of them, mostly due to the fact that their idea of what a feminist is has been tainted by incorrect stereotypes or false media depictions. At the end of the day, a feminist is someone who simply advocates for equality of the sexes, a notion that doesn't seem too outlandish.

Despite these life-changing efforts for equality, it seems the perception of feminism has changed. People hear the word "feminist" and don't think of the Seneca Falls Convention or Betty Friedan or Elizabeth Cady Stanton. Today, the typical American associates feminism with all of the lies that the media has told them; feminists are bitter, man-hating, and fighting a battle that has already been won. Opposers of feminism take one glance at women's history and minimalize its significance, boiling the feminist movement down to a couple of unruly, bitter women.

THE NEGATIVE PERCEPTION

Why the negative perception? What exactly is the negative perception? Where did it come from? The negative perception of feminism explains the experience I witnessed in my college class.

The word feminism in today's world seems like a curse word or used as an insult.

People correlate feminism with the idea that men are the culprit for women's challenges in society. While this is somewhat true, the resulting stigma around the movement is harmful. As a result, many people reject feminism for different reasons. Many people reject the "feminist" label because they don't want to carry around the burden of being associated with the word's negative connotations. In their minds, it's easier to believe in feminist ideas than it is to proudly pronounce one's association with the feminist movement.

In particular, the belief that feminists are extremists who seek to exterminate men must end. Many males do have this thought regarding feminism, and thus, see it as a threat. It is wrongfully assumed that being a feminist means wanting to push all men out of power and have women control the world. Much anti-feminist hate speech refers to the idea that feminism is in pursuit of making women superior, instead of equal, to men. It is essential to realize the true goals of feminists–which is solely leveling the playing field for both sexes. It must be noted that women are not pursuing sameness. We are seeking equality.

In the 1920s, identifying as a feminist entailed a different experience. These feminists faced speculation about their sexual preferences. Female supporters (wrongfully) were characterized as militant, anti-male, and hostile humans. Antifeminism groups were identified as early as the first wave of feminism when men feared that a more liberated woman would violate the natural order of things as prescribed in religious texts. It was also believed that family values would be demolished and traditional motherhood would cease to exist. The pro-family movement of the 19th century opposed the idea of women's liberation, stating that the nation could only remain strong if households upheld the outdated ideas of what a family looked like. The National League for the Protection of the Family served as one of the main opposers to feminist ideas. Founder Samuel Dike insisted that a family must have "one man and one woman, united in wedlock, together with their children."

It is important to note that many leaders of the movement against women's suffrage were actually women themselves. Though they routinely encouraged women to explore realms outside of the home, they were opposed to the idea of women entering the world of politics. Antisuffragists believed that women already had enough going on without getting involved in legislation and laws. They also feared that being able to vote would force women to choose an alignment to a political party, which would dispose of their usual nonpartisanship. Antifeminism was further fueled during the Cold War. In 1951, a novel titled *Washington Confidential* was published. The misogynistic, racist, and homophobic novel linked feminism and the employment of people of color and queer people to Communism, implying that the "white, Christian, heterosexual, patriarchal family" was the only type of family that could help to put an end to the Cold War.

As I stated earlier, the Equal Rights Amendment sought to keep all laws on equal playing grounds for both men and women. The official wording of the ERA is as follows: "Equality of rights under the law shall not be denied or abridged by the United States or by any state on account of sex." Seems pretty reasonable, right? Not to some people. Not even an amendment banning gender discrimination was safe from the opposition of antifeminists. The main adversaries of the Equal Rights Amendment were women who sought to maintain traditional gender roles. They cultivated fear by explaining how the Equal Rights Amendment would force women to go off to fight in the war, eliminate gendered bathrooms, and allow for the admittance of men into women's colleges. The leader of the Stop ERA group was conservative activist Phyllis Schlafly, who used working women's fears of a war draft to manipulate them into rallying against the Equal Rights Amendment's ratification. She preyed upon the women who were housewives, convincing them that they'd be forced to leave the home and be left to the mercy of the job market, a market for which they possessed no practical skills or knowledge or connections.

Schlafly caught the public's eye after the publication of *A Choice Not an Echo*, a non-fiction book in which Schlafly explores the process of presidential nominations and elections. Prior to the Equal Rights Amendment ordeal, Schlafly ran for and subsequently lost Illinois's 23rd congressional district to Democratic candidate George E. Shipley. She then turned her attention away from running for public office and towards putting an end to the "feminist agenda" and the Equal Rights Amendment. After slowing down the ratification of the Equal Rights Amendment, Schlafly kept her name in the news by voicing her controversial opinions on Roe v. Wade, marital rape, and the United Nations. She endorsed Donald Trump for the 2016 presidential election before passing away at the age of 92, a day before the publication of her final work, *The Conservative Case for Trump*. Schlafly's arguments against the feminist-backed equality legislation proved effective and led to decreased support for the Equal Rights Amendment. "Many people who followed the struggle over the ERA believed—rightly in my view—that the Amendment would have been ratified by 1975 or 1976 had it not been for Phyllis Schlafly's early and effective effort to organize potential opponents," said political scientist Jane Mansbridge.

Conservative religious groups were also to blame for many people's reservations when it came to the Equal Rights Amendment. Organizations and religious branches such as The Church of Jesus Christ of Latter-day Saints and Roman Catholics fervently opposed the Equal Rights Amendment because they believed that it would increase the number of abortions and encourage same-sex marriages. Though the Equal Rights Amendment wasn't completely ratified back in 1972, strides have been made in recent years to get the ERA ratified in all states.

Feminists are often associated with the bra-burning incident, which was later proven to be a myth. The misconception that feminists are crazy bra-burners originated at the Miss America protest that occurred on September 7, 1968. A group of feminists called the New York Radical Women, founded by former child actress Robin Morgan, Carol Hanisch, Shulamith Firestone, and Pam Allen, decided to stage a demonstration at the Atlantic City boardwalk in hopes of bringing attention to the sexist, derogatory, and oppressive nature of beauty pageants. After seeing how participants in the pageant had to walk around the stage in swimsuits, Hanisch got the idea to protest the Miss America pageant. "It got me thinking that protesting the pageant might be a good way to launch the movement into the public consciousness," said Hanisch. "Because up until this time, we hadn't done a lot of actions yet. We were a very small movement. It was kind of a gutsy thing to do. Miss America was this 'American pie' icon. Who would dare criticize this?"

So, on September 7th, 1968, a group of around 400 women from cities around the eastern U.S. marched on the Atlantic City boardwalk. They passed out pamphlets and carried posters that brought attention to the oppressiveness and harmfulness of beauty pageants. The bra-burning myth originated from a part of the protest called the "Freedom Trash Can," in which feminist participants would throw traditionally feminine items like high-heels, false eyelashes, and yes, bras. However, all of the women who participated in the event denied claims that they had burned any of the things in the wastebasket. When asked whether or not bras were burned that day, protest organizer Hanisch said, "We had intended to burn it, but the police department, since we were on the boardwalk, wouldn't let us do the burning."

There were contradicting reports from that day in which specta-tors said that they did, in fact, witness the feminists burning their bras, but that the fire was brief and extinguished quickly. Never-theless, the association of feminists with the burning of bras has persisted to this day and carries with it a negative connotation. The narrative of angry bra-burning feminists has been used to invalidate and minimize what the protest was aiming to accom-plish. Anti-feminists have used the incident to attack the feminist movement, accusing the pageant demonstrators of only protest-ing so that they could attract the attention of men.

It's interesting to note that, on the same day of September 7th, 1968, a separate protest surrounding Miss America took place. Only this time, demonstrators participated and competed in an actual beauty pageant. This demonstration was the very first Miss Black America pageant, in which black women were finally able to participate in a beauty pageant. "Miss America does not represent us because there has never been a black girl in the pageant. With my title, I can show black women that they too are beautiful," stated the pageant's first-ever winner Saundra Williams. The use of the beauty pageant as a way to take a stand against the racism and discrimination faced by black women shows the complexity and interconnectedness of feminism and racism in America. Yet, these stereotypes still carry weight today.

Unsurprisingly, the male gaze views feminists as bitter. They assume that these women cannot attract a husband. If a woman could not get a man, they must be resentful or a lesbian. Deeply sexist anti-feminist propaganda depicts feminists as unattractive, masculine, and emotional. When feminists were fighting for the right to vote, men were publishing cartoons of what they imagined a world of voting women would look like; in one of the anti-suffrage postcards, a group of women sits around a table, cigars in hand, while a man cares for a child in the background. One of the women tells her friends, "My old man is a lazy old wretch!" A sign on the wall reads, "Notice to Fathers: Wash Your Shirts with Sud's Soap." The postcard is titled, "When Women Vote," and served as a warning to a world where men were forced to *shudder* take care of their own children.

According to the beliefs of antifeminists, feminists do not come across as feminine. They have hairy legs and underarms, go out bare-faced rather than wearing makeup, and lack the grooming skills that only women who don't identify as feminists are able to possess. They believe that feminists reject all forms of femininity. After all, if feminists are trying to become men, what's to stop them from looking like them, too? Antifeminists have also convinced themselves that feminists must be misandrists as well, when, in reality, all feminists are doing is holding men accountable for their actions. Feminists are fighting for equality so that they can be masculine, feminine, have long hair, paint their nails, and just be able to do whatever they want to do with their bodies. Nevertheless, there are many women who would rather stray away from a movement which would make them 'man-haters' and these other accusations.

The lack of participation from men comes from this idea that feminist movements removes a woman's femininity. Men assume that identifying as a feminist removes their masculine nature. They believe that feminists will reject everything considered feminine, such as shaved legs, makeup, and other forms of grooming. They also assume that women who identify as feminists will never want to be stay-at-home moms or can't be religious. However, these gender associations are just a construct. There is no scale to measure how masculine or feminine a person is. There really is no need for one. If anything, a man being an ally for women makes them more attractive.

WHAT CREATED THIS NEGATIVE PERCEPTION?

Of course, there is not one person or instance to blame for these associations with feminism. Rather, the root of these negative perceptions is the misjudged. Anti-women propaganda changes the main aim of feminism. In other words, they make the public believe feminism means hating men.

A prevalent criticism against the feminist movement is that it doesn't advocate for men's issues. This simply isn't true. Feminists have historically fought to see pro-LGBTQ+ laws passed, and have continuously been outspoken about their support for the LGBTQ + community, which consists of men, women, and everyone in between. In addition, feminists helped to enact the Prison Rape Elimination Act of 2003, which seeks to "eradicate prisoner rape in all types of correctional facilities in this country." In 2012, feminists played a major role in changing the federal definition of rape so that it included all genders. Until then, rape was defined as something that could only happen to females. Also, breaking free of gender roles and stereotypes doesn't just benefit women. It benefits men as well. Men should be able to pursue professions typically associated with women, such as teaching, nursing, and homemaking, without feeling less manly. The fight against domestic violence also benefits victims who identify as male. In 1994, The National Organization for Women played a key role in passing the Violence Against Women Act. Despite having only women in the title, the act also protects men who are victims of domestic and other forms of violence.

Our society sees extreme feminist groups on the news, yet, does no further research on the underlying causes. Those who have already made their minds up about feminism stay put in their echo chambers, never making the effort to learn all the good that feminism has done for both men and women since ancient times. In short, the crave for power on behalf of white males misconstrues the goals of feminism. White men have seen their power trickling away into the hands of women, and they are not happy. In portraying feminist movements in this narrative, both men and women gain a wrongful sense of feminist goals.

Feminists are often demonized in the media. They are portrayed as sexually deviant, rageful monsters who hate men and want to destroy family values. And, when they are shown, they're mostly placed in the context of marches, rallies, and protests (not to say that these are bad things), which further distances feminists from "normal" women and pushes the idea that you can be a feminist or a homemaker, but not both. Of course, most of the people who decide what gets published in mass media are men seeking to maintain their power over women, and they often think that by portraying feminists as less-than-human, the fight for equality of the sexes will be slowed down, keeping their positions of power safely out of women's reach.

Additionally, this view only represents such a small group in the movement. In a study on feminism for minorities, the majority of minorities acknowledged that feminist movements did do something for them. However, present concerns of feminism feel more geared to the challenges faced by white women.

*There are so many different organizations that help marginal-
ized groups and additionally, focus on safety and the advancement for women around the world.*

Before moving on, I want to take a quick dive into the history of
feminism as it relates to marginalized groups. As previously mentioned, feminism has disproportionately benefited white women.
This brand of "white feminism" has been a major criticism of the
feminist movement since the first wave in 1848 and has helped
create the negative perception that feminism only helps white college-educated women. White feminism focuses on the struggles
and concerns of white women while neglecting the issues faced
by women of color, women of the religious minority, transgender
and queer women, and women of low class or status. Each wave
has been afflicted by its unique brand of white feminism, which
slows down the feminist movement as a whole while also imped-
ing the advancement of marginalized groups. Though we have
come far when it comes to the intersectionality of feminism, there
are still strides to be made in terms of the inclusion of *all* women.

First-wave feminism, which centered on securing the right for
women to vote, largely benefited white women. When the 19th
amendment was ratified, not all women were guaranteed a trip
to the polls. There were still legal barriers that needed to be over-
come. Qualifications such as literacy tests and poll taxes greatly
disenfranchised black men and women, not to mention the racism, Jim Crow laws, and threats of hate crimes that came with
venturing to different parts of town. Some states even enacted
laws that were meant to keep women from voting. After the
19th amendment's ratification, Georgia passed a law that severely
impacted women's ability to vote: "Many negro women have regis-
tered here since the suffrage amendment became effective. The
election judges ruled that they were not entitled to vote because of
a state law which requires registration six months before an election." So, right off the bat, women were facing unfair pushback

from lawmakers regarding their voting status.

Black men and women proved vital to the suffrage movement. Legendary American educator Fannie Barrier Williams founded a "sufferage school" at St. Louis' Young Women's Christian Association, which prepared and familiarized women of color with all voting processes. Mary Jane McLeod Bethune was also a vital leader of the black suffrage movement. The civil rights activist did everything in her power to get black women to the polls, organizing donation drives to pay poll taxes, providing education related to the ballots, and making sure that all women passed their literacy tests. Thanks to her valiant efforts, black women showed up to the polls like never before.

Princess Sophia Alexandrovna Duleep Singh was a famous Sikh Indian suffragette who helped to advance voting rights for women in the United Kingdom. Singh used her title as Princess to persuade prominent politicians to help further the suffrage movement. She led marches and protests, held meetings to discuss the unfair practices of the British government, and regularly sold a newspaper called *The Suffragette* outside of Hampton Court Palace.

Prominent suffragettes Elizabeth Cady Stanton and Susan B. Anthony were major culprits of white feminism. In 1876, they initiated a project titled *History of Woman Suffrage*, in which the women would detail the events of the suffrage movement. The problem was that Stanton and Anthony focused solely on white suffragettes. The 5,700-page book provides very limited coverage of groups outside of Stanton and Anthony's and virtually no information on marginalized women's fight for the right to vote.

Mary Church Terrel was another important figure of the suffrage movement. Terrel was one of the few African-American women allowed to attend National American Woman Suffrage Association meetings, and she used her attendance to speak on the various issues faced by black women when it came to casting a vote in elections. Terrel addressed members of the National American Woman Suffrage Association at their 15th-anniversary celebration in a speech titled "The Progress of Colored Women."

"When one considers the obstacles encountered by colored women in their effort to educate and cultivate themselves, since they became free, the work they have accomplished and the progress they have made will bear favorable comparison, at least with that of their more fortunate sisters, from whom the opportunity of acquiring knowledge and the means of self-culture have never been entirely withheld," begins Terrel. "Not only are colored women with ambition and aspiration handicapped on account of their sex, but they are almost everywhere baffled and mocked because of their race. Not only because they are women, but because they are colored women, are discouragement and disappointment meeting them at every turn. But in spite of the obstacles encountered, the progress made by colored women along many lines appears like a veritable miracle of modern times." In this opening section of her speech, Terrel directly addresses the privilege that white women have due to the color of their skin. She further points to the indispensability of intersectional feminism, stating that black women must face the challenges that accompany being a woman as well as the challenges posed by being a person of color.

As with first-wave feminism, second-wave feminism tended to leave marginalized women out of the conversation. Once again, middle-class white women held the microphone, and they shouted over women who experienced barriers posed by race, sexuality, and class status. Activist bell hooks was an important leader of second-wave feminism, advocating for the liberation of black women. In her work *Feminist Theory: From Margin to Center* hooks discusses what it means to be both a feminist and a member of a marginalized group: "Women in lower class and poor groups, particularly those who are non-white, would not have defined women's liberation as women gaining social equality with men since they are continually reminded in their everyday lives that all women do not share a common social status."

Third-wave feminism improved immensely when it came to intersectionality, mostly due to the fact that one of the wave's major goals was to make feminism inclusive of all women's experiences. Intersectionality, or the lack thereof, was discussed more broadly in major feminist circles. Nevertheless, the absence of intersectionality is still a hot button issue and is one of the reasons that some people, mostly women, believe that feminism is viewed negatively.

Social media also has a major impact on feminism. In fact, you can find an example of an anti-feminism quote easily. With the power of social media, a wave of ignorance resulted in misinformation. Phenomena such as echo chambers and confirmation bias cause people to only be exposed to one viewpoint, which means that they will be very stubborn when it comes to listening to others. In 2014, a Twitter account known as "Meninist Page" was created and had a following of over 1 million followers. The page specifically designated a space to make fun of women, push chauvinistic ideas, and bring down the idea of the feminist movement. It's not just men who have used social media to discount the ideas of feminism. There is a social media movement called Women Against Feminism where women share their reasoning behind opposing feminism, usually by taking a selfie with a hand-written sign stating "I don't need feminism because…" This harmful movement originated in 2013 and has been plaguing social media sites like Twitter and Tumblr ever since.

Antifeminist organizations like Women Against Feminism have been around since the beginning of the feminist movement. While they don't claim to be against gender equality, they generally believe that equality has already been achieved and that feminism is no longer needed. They have fallen into the trap that the mass media has laid for them: feminism is about gaining superiority, not equality, over men. They don't want the negative connotations that come with being labeled as a feminist. Some even believe that feminism will make men's lives more difficult. In a Women Against Feminism blog post, one suporter wrote: "I'm anti feminist because it is unfair to men, but also because it is unfair to women. I don't have a son yet but I might be pregnant with a boy this time and I am afraid of the life that he will have. I am afraid of how badly our culture treats males. I am afraid of what his future wife can do to him."

Other groups like Return of Kings and A Voice for Men have voiced their misogynistic views on their blogs. There was even a blog post circulating in 2017 in which the author, Roosh, wrote that women's suffrage needed to be repealed, insisting that "Because they don't operate on logic like men do, you will always have this destructive element within the political ranks of your nation as long as women have the right to vote." Nope, this isn't satire. He actually believes that all of the problems in America can be fixed if women are banned from voting. The worst part is, everyone in the comment section agreed! The encouraging, supportive replies underneath this blog post are a reminder that misogyny is more prevalent than ever in today's society.

As a result, these pages spread the idea that women are crazy man-haters. Additionally, the double standards between men and women are seen as fictional or over-exaggerated. To make matters worse, the "Meninist Page" was not the only account to spread these ideas. The widespread effects of social media influenced a lot of people. It ruined the general mindset on the topic for both men and some women. If women bought into the idea that feminism is wrong, it is clear that social media ruined the entire purpose and the effectiveness of the movement.

It is crucial that people of all genders be taught to conduct their own research regarding feminism. There are too many biased depictions and accounts of the meaning of feminism that don't align with what feminism actually is: the advocacy of equality. It's as simple as that. Labels aren't everything, but not identifying as a feminist because of the false stereotypes presented by the media is harmful in the fight for true equality of the sexes, a fight that everyone, regardless of their background, should be participating in.

MY PERSONAL EXPERIENCE

I was a feminist before I knew what feminism was. To be a feminist simply means that I believed that women are capable of anything. I grew up in a household where the difference between treatment on the basis of sex was clear. Being a feminist is actually a really wonderful thing to be regardless of one's gender.

This was easy for me to admit because I am an attractive black straight woman, who wants better for other black women.

I grew up in an environment that valued women and their contributions. Women were never seen as inferior to men, and my sisters and I were often encouraged to pursue any career path that we were passionate about, regardless of if it was typically male-dominated. I didn't understand what it meant to be a feminist until entering the collegiate world and being exposed to academia. I had certainly heard about feminists and their fight for equality, but I wasn't aware of its history or how it related to race, class, and sexuality. In my film classes, we examined important feminist films and directors. In my economics classes, we talked about women's role in monumental economic events like the Great Depression. In my communications and technology class, we talked about the role mass media plays in prejudices and discrimination, including the hatred for women. Despite the opposition that some of my relatives or friends might have to the word, all of my college-education and personal research has led me to believe that I am, in fact, a feminist.

As a white, college-educated woman, it's important to acknowledge how my whiteness grants me privileges that women of color don't have. It is also vital that I use my privilege to amplify and listen to the voices of minority women. Though it was never intentional, I am guilty of not doing enough research when it comes to struggles that women who don't identify as white and straight have faced. Passing the mic to less privileged women is essential if we as a society want to reach the point of complete intersectionality.

Our discussion of the different waves of feminism helped get women to where we are today. There is still so much work to be done–especially for minority women. Creating change is as simple as raising our daughters to believe they are capable of anything. For, we live in a world that wasn't created for minorities to succeed in. As a new 21st century feminist movement arises, we must extend the benefits of second-wave feminism and third-wave feminism to aid in equality.

AFTERWORD

Stereotypes can be restricting, and we understand acting accordingly to stray away from them. However, these feminist stereotypes will still exist. There will always be those who genuinely believe that feminists are men-hating, unattractive monsters who are fighting a nonexistent battle. However, we can do our part in reducing the number of people who believe in the stereotypes. It is important to stand your ground when it comes to fighting for equality, no matter what others may think. In other words, you will still be called ugly, a man-hater, and so on, for not giving men the attention they crave. So, if you can still be considered bitter (or even assumed as a lesbian if you choose to be single), we are left with the question: what do you really have to lose?

www.ingramcontent.com/pod-product-compliance
Lightning Source LLC
Chambersburg PA
CBHW061545250726
48657CB00006B/2304